SIMON & SCHUSTER BOOKS FOR YOUNG READERS • An imprint of Simon & Schuster Children's Publishing Division • 1230 Avenue of the Americas, New York, New York 10020 • Copyright © 2015 by Meghan McCarthy • All rights reserved, including the right of reproduction in whole or in part in any form. • SIMON & SCHUSTER BOOKS FOR YOUNG READERS is a trademark of Simon & Schuster, Inc. • For information about special discounts for bulk purchases, please contact Simon & Schuster Special Sales at 1-866-506-1949 or business@simonandschuster.com. • The Simon & Schuster Speakers Bureau can bring authors to your live event. For more information or to book an event, contact the Simon & Schuster Speakers Bureau at 1-866-248-3049 or visit our website at www.simonspeakers.com. • Book design by Chloë Foglia • The text for this book is set in Caxton. • The illustrations for this book are rendered in acrylic paint. • Manufactured in China • 0815 SCP   10 9 8 7 6 5 4 3   • Library of Congress Cataloging-in-Publication Data • McCarthy, Meghan, author. • Earmuffs for everyone! : how Chester Greenwood became known as the inventor of earmuffs / Meghan McCarthy. • pages cm • "A Paula Wiseman Book." • Summary: "This picture book biography of Chester Greenwood explores the invention of the earmuffs and the patenting process"—Provided by publisher. • ISBN 978-1-4814-0637-6 (hardback) — ISBN 978-1-4814-0638-3 (eBook) • 1. Greenwood, Chester, 1858-1937—Juvenile literature. 2. Inventors—Maine—Farmington—Juvenile literature. 3. Earmuffs—Juvenile literature. 4. Patents—Juvenile literature. I. Title. • T40.G67M33 2015 • 687'.4—dc23 • [B] • 2014020159

EARMUFFS
— for —
EVERYONE!

How Chester Greenwood Became
Known as the Inventor of Earmuffs

By Meghan McCarthy

A PAULA WISEMAN BOOK
Simon & Schuster Books for Young Readers
New York   London   Toronto   Sydney   New Delhi

The word "muff" has been around since the Middle Ages. Starting in the 1700s, people wore muffs on their hands to keep them warm, like this:

In the 1800s, hand muffs looked like this:

In 1858, William Ware invented one of the first kinds of earmuffs, called "ear, cheek, and chin muffs."

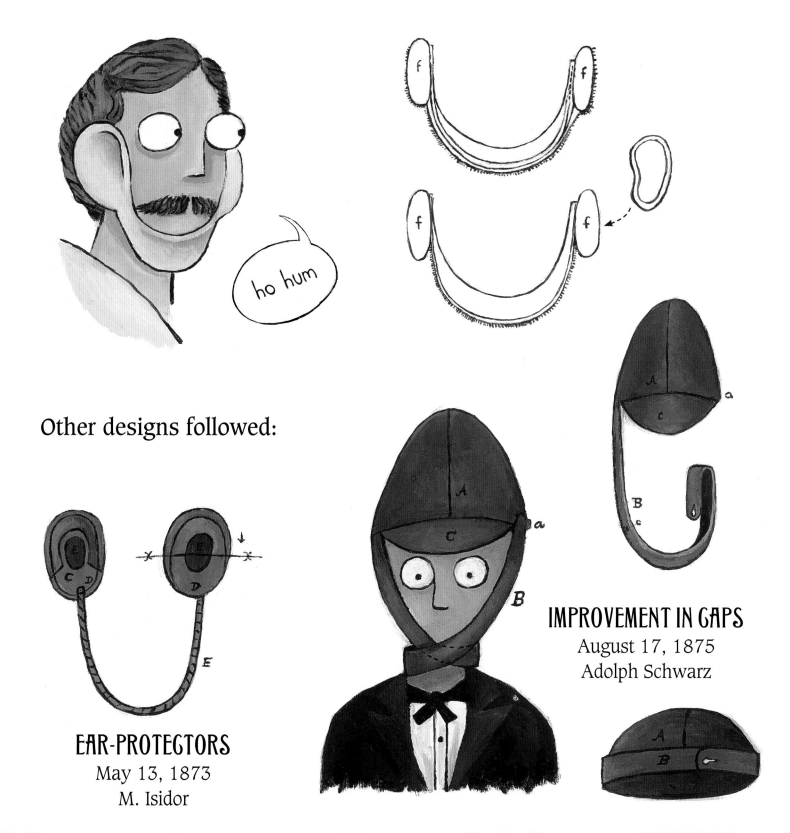

Other designs followed:

EAR-PROTECTORS
May 13, 1873
M. Isidor

IMPROVEMENT IN CAPS
August 17, 1875
Adolph Schwarz

EAR-SLIPPERS
May 15, 1877
I. B. Kleinert

CAP AND COLLAR COMBINED
April 9, 1878
M. Isidor

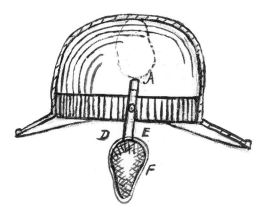

EAR PROTECTOR
June 26, 1883
C. Beard and
C. E. Baldwin

Another inventor named Isaac Kleinert placed ads in major newspapers to promote his ear protectors.

Kleinert made other things too—mostly out of rubber. He made waterproof baby pants. He also made dress guards, which protected ladies' clothing from sweat. Ew!

Believe it or not, his company exists today! *You* can still buy a pair of sweat protectors!

But the guy everyone knows as the inventor of earmuffs is Chester Greenwood.

CHESTER GREENWOOD AS AN ADULT

As the story goes, he had gigantic ears, and they were sensitive to the cold. He didn't like to wrap his head in scratchy scarves, so . . .

CHESTER GREENWOOD AS A BOY

he ran home to Granny and asked her to fashion some ear covers out of wire and cloth.

Earmuffs were born.

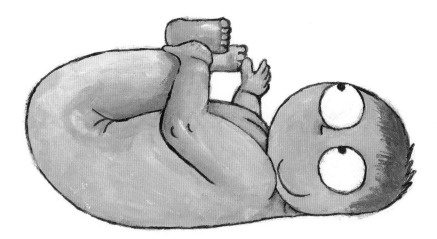

Obviously, the story isn't quite true, since earmuffs had already been born many years earlier—four months before Chester was! And there is another story that says Chester didn't like the woolen earmuffs that most kids wore, so he fashioned something else.

What do you think really happened?

What we do know for sure is that after testing various versions of his earmuffs, when Chester was just nineteen, he got one of these from the US government:

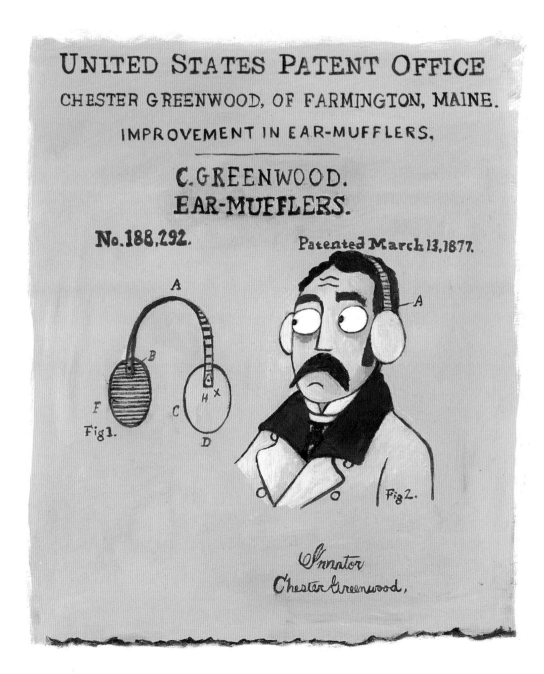

It's a patent! I know what you're thinking: Just what *is* a patent?

Patents are issued by the US Patent Office. When Chester was a boy, the office building in Washington, DC, looked like this:

A patent allows the inventor the sole right to make, use, or sell something. It means that no one but the inventor can make money from it!

Here are some famous patented inventions.

COKE BOTTLES

BAND-AIDS

SCOTCH TAPE

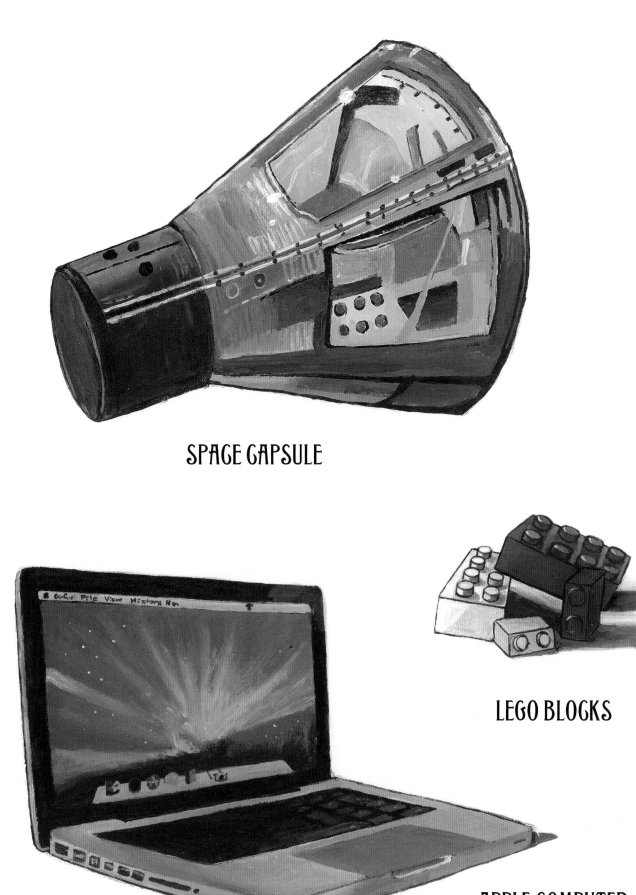

SPACE CAPSULE

LEGO BLOCKS

APPLE COMPUTER

Before Chester's earmuffs came along, earmuffs didn't fit snugly to the ears. Chester came up with a tight steel band that held those mufflers in place! *That* is what Chester did for earmuffs. He made people's ears even warmer.

It's just like the story of Thomas Edison and the lightbulb:

THOMAS EDISON,
FAMOUS INVENTOR

These inventions came before Edison's. But before Edison, lightbulbs didn't stay lit for long. One of Edison's early lightbulbs lasted for forty hours. That was a big improvement. Edison didn't invent the lightbulb. He made it better. That is what Chester did for the earmuff.

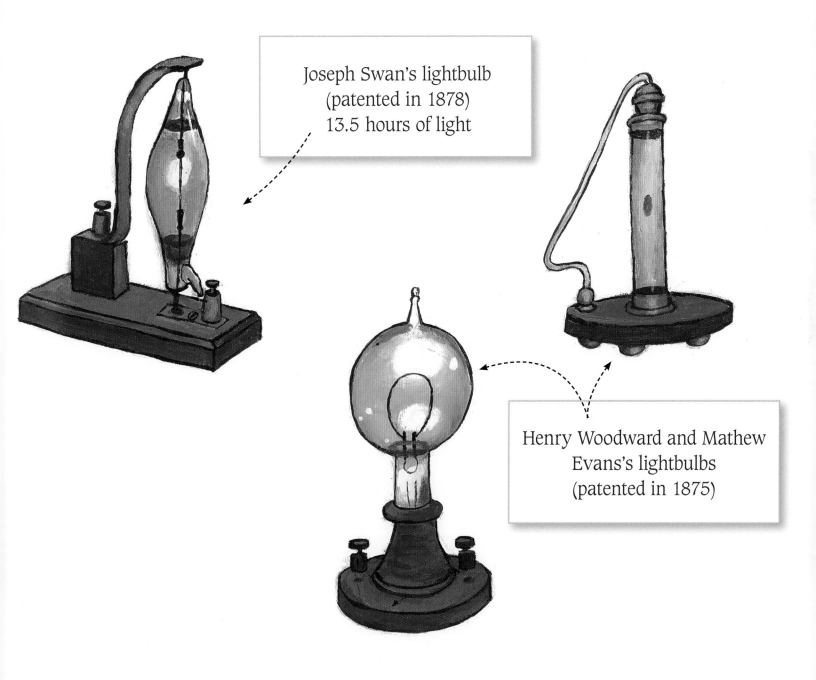

Joseph Swan's lightbulb
(patented in 1878)
13.5 hours of light

Henry Woodward and Mathew Evans's lightbulbs
(patented in 1875)

Back to the story of Chester Greenwood:
It is said that when Chester was a boy he was already thinking about how he could earn money. He went door to door selling eggs he got from his family's chickens. With the profits from the eggs he bought candy. Most kids would have eaten the candy . . . but not Chester—he sold it!
Even as a boy, he was practicing good business skills.

It was those good business skills that helped the young Chester sell his ear protectors as far off as Canada.

Soon he earned enough money to buy a wonderful home for his family. It sat high on a hill overlooking the town and river.

And it was said that he had the first steam car in town.

Chester also had a workshop in town. On the top floor was his earmuff factory. Below it was his bicycle shop.

Chester didn't just invent earmuffs. He worked on other products as well. Here are a few of his improvements:

"ROUND BOTTOM" TEA KETTLE
(Chester rounded the edges to reduce wear and make the kettle last longer.)

UMBRELLA BAG
(To hold umbrellas—this was not patented.)

RAKE
(The rake was metal and had removable parts so when a "tooth" broke, the owner could put a new one in, instead of having to buy a whole new rake.)

And then there's this "portable" house, which could be easily built and taken apart.

Would you want to take this camping?

While Chester was busy with his business, his wife, Isabel, was busy with her own affairs. She had joined the Maine chapter of the Women's Suffrage Movement. The Suffrage Movement was a women's rights movement.

One of its main goals was to get women the right to vote.
Women were not able to vote in the late 1800s. Isabel held
meetings at their house on the hill. Perhaps this is why Chester
employed so many women at his factory.

In 1937 Chester Greenwood passed away. Soon after his death his factory closed for good. But Chester would not be forgotten.

What's interesting is that by 1939, people seemed to remember Chester and forget about all the other earmuff inventors. An article in *Life* magazine read:

BEAUTY AND FASHION COME TO THE LOWLY EARMUFF

Earmuffs were invented sixty-four years ago by the late Chester Greenwood, a Farmington Falls, Maine, lad with sensitive ears. For nearly sixty years he was the sole purveyor of earmuffs to postmen, policemen, farmers, and country boys. He had only one style, like the Model-T Ford—black, utilitarian, unlovely. The market was almost exclusively male. Then, four years ago, skiers and college girls made them fashionable. . . .

They only remembered Chester. To them, *he* was the inventor of earmuffs.

Many people wanted his legacy to live on. In the 1970s, a man named Mickey Maguire, who worked at a newsstand, thought there should be a Chester Greenwood Day.

To drum up excitement, Mickey made up some stories. Mickey said that Chester woke up at four a.m. and ran a mile to the factory to light the boilers.

"I couldn't remember what was true and what was not," said Mickey's friend, a journalist. "I still can't. I'm afraid that I told . . . some terrible, wicked yarns."

Chester Greenwood Day
went all the way to the Maine
legislature. The congressmen
argued back and forth. Some
wanted the day. Some thought it
was silly! One senator said, "Now
we've roped the national media into giving
us publicity, let's kill it." Another senator
disagreed, saying, "I predict that every December 21,
Maine will be back in the news." After much disagreement,
Chester Greenwood Day was official in 1977!

Every year Chester Greenwood Day is celebrated in December.

There are people and buses and cars . . .
all wearing earmuffs. Everyone has a good
time. Chester is celebrated each year as the
inventor of earmuffs.

And that's how the story goes. Chester may not have created the original earmuff . . . but he made it better. Sometimes that's what makes all the difference.

A Note about This Book

I start work on every book with a bit of free association. For *Earmuffs* I started doing searches on the Internet—"unique inventors," "odd inventions"—until ultimately I put in the words "kid inventors." That's when I read about Chester Greenwood, who was born in 1858. Mary Bellis of About.com wrote, "A grammar school dropout, he invented earmuffs at the age of 15 (1873). While testing a new pair of ice skates, he grew frustrated at trying to protect his ears from the bitter cold. . . ." That's when I knew that Chester was going to be the topic of my next book. What I didn't know was how hard it would be to extract the truth from the fiction.

Wikipedia lists Chester Greenwood as the inventor of the earmuff, but since it's an open-source site it's not a reliable source of information. More established sources such as National Public Radio and the *Washington Post* also list Chester Greenwood as the inventor of earmuffs. But something didn't seem right to me. The top of Chester's original earmuff patent reads "Improvement in ear-mufflers." I wondered about this. What was meant by "Improvement"? Did Chester have a patent before this? I went searching for an answer but was sent in circles. I finally found my answer while digging through old advertisements. Staring at me was an ad for earmuffs from 1875 that pre-dated Chester's patent. The earmuffs were created by Isaac Kleinert from New York City. The NYC Science, Industry, and Business Library confirmed my suspicion that Chester Greenwood was not the original inventor of earmuffs. I then found dozens of earmuff patents, all with different names—head-muffs, ear-protectors, ear-mufflers, ear-flaps, ear slippers . . . They all had one thing in common: They were all competing for buyers' attention in the late 1800s.

I thought there was still a story there . . . it was just a different one. Somewhere along the line the other inventors were forgotten. How did this happen? And what made Chester Greenwood unique enough that all of Maine celebrates him to this day?

Chester Greenwood

Chester Greenwood may not have been the first inventor of earmuffs, but he was possibly the youngest. This, in itself, is a feat. It's quite ambitious of any teenager to acquire a patent for something he or she has designed. What may have made Chester's design unique was the steel headband that fit the earmuffs snugly on the ears. I purchased a pair of Victorian earmuffs and they contained all of the same components as Chester's except for one thing. The pair I purchased seemed floppy. I could not determine how they would sit snugly. From what I could gather, after Chester released his patent, other earmuffs advertising steel headbands began to appear. I assume that Chester had his idea first. Back then the patent process was tit for tat. One inventor came up with something and then another inventor did the same thing or something remarkably similar. Computer systems didn't exist yet, so it was much harder to check for too-similar products.

I suspect Chester is known as the inventor of earmuffs because he died last. The other inventors were much older than he was. The first written mention of Chester as the inventor of earmuffs that I could find was in his obituary. Fast-forward to the mid-1970s and the facts got muddled, as one reporter even admitted. So what can we trust when everyone who knew Chester is dead and the newspapers and magazines since the 1940s reported inaccuracies? Well . . . not a heck of a lot.

Newspapers during Chester's life didn't produce much about him, but that's not surprising since during his lifetime he was not known as the inventor of the earmuff. Although he was not a grammar school dropout, as About.com states, it is true he did not seek further education. It was obviously unnecessary, as Chester was quite the entrepreneur. He owned a telephone business and a boat shop, among other ventures. For a list of Chester Greenwood's inventions, go to my website, meghan-mccarthy.com/earmuffs.html.

What sources agree on is that Chester had the inventor spirit. Although his other inventions didn't amount to much, Chester never stopped tinkering, and it's that innate curiosity that made him special. I think the lesson is that you don't have to be the next Thomas Edison to leave a mark. Since it's a bit unclear as to who the very first person was to invent the earmuff, ear-muffler, ear slipper, ear wrapping, or ear covering, Chester Greenwood is a good person to represent them all . . . don't you think?

All about Patents

Let's say you imagine the coolest time machine ever. You draw up your plans and decide to patent it, so that no one else can come up with the same idea and make money from it. Think again! You cannot patent something that will not actually work! Now let's say you invent something that *does* work: a clock radio that also toasts bread every morning. You create designs for the clock-radio-toaster and make a working model. When you apply for a patent, your patent will protect your invention for twenty years. After twenty years it is no longer protected, and other people can copy your invention.

When you apply for a patent, you must provide a detailed description of your invention. This will be in a searchable database that is available to the public. Because of the public accessibility, many companies that wish to keep their products private, such as Coca-Cola, will not apply for a patent so that they can keep the details of their inventions a secret. Because Coke's recipe is unique and the company does not wish it to be copied, they would rather not risk applying for a patent, because after the twenty years are up, everyone would be able to copy their soda's magic recipe!

But *you* have decided it's worth the risk to patent your invention. Be prepared for a long process!

The first thing you must do is hire a patent attorney. After that you must gather all the sketches and art created for your clock-radio-toaster. Then you must write up a summary of your invention. Next you must create a detailed drawing of your clock-radio-toaster

and write a legal description of your invention. Now be prepared for how expensive your lawyer might be—anywhere from $5,000 to $20,000! Make sure that your clock-radio-toaster will make far more profit than your lawyer's fee!

After your application is complete, it is sent to the US Patent Office. This costs several hundred dollars in fees. At this point your patent will be called "pending." Cross your fingers and hope that it is approved. Good luck!

To learn more, visit the US Patent and Trademark Office online at uspto.gov.

A parade celebrating Chester Greenwood Day that takes place every December in Farmington, Maine.

Credit: Scott Landry

Bibliography

News Articles

Bangor Daily News. "House votes (Earmuff) Greenwood Day." May 21, 1977.

Boston Post. "Maine Man Invented Spring Earlaps." March 25, 1934.

Chicago Tribune. "Earmuffs." February 16, 1988.

Corbett, Christopher. "The Awful Truth about Chester Greenwood." *Yankee*, December 1977.

Curran, Jeanne. "Unique Earmuff Collection Part of Lore of Maine." *Bangor Daily News*, January 10, 1990.

Davis, Greg. "Chester Greenwood Was a Leading Local Citizen Then and Now." *Franklin Journal*, November 28, 2000.

Fortune. "Earmuffs." February 1937.

Garboden, Clif. "Primer: Earmuffs." *Boston Globe Magazine*, February 18, 1990.

Jespersen, Betty. "Libraries Joining Parade for Earmuff Inventor." *Kennebec Journal*, December 1, 2007.

Kansas City Times. "Residents Honor Inventor of Earmuffs with Wear-in." December 22, 1987.

Lewiston Daily Sun. "Farmington Honors Earmuff Inventor." December 22, 1987.

Lewiston Journal. "Farmington Boy's Sensitive Ears Were His Fortune." February 27, 1926.

Moody, Sid. "Muffed-up in Maine." *Lawrence Journal-World*, February 18, 1988.

New York Herald Tribune. "Greenwood, 78, Dies; Invented Ear Muff at 15." July 8, 1937.

New York Post. "If Winter Comes . . . Remember Chester Greenwood." July 23, 1937.

Portland Maine Press Herald. "Mr. Greenwood." July 11, 1937.

Wall Street Journal. "Chester's Cold Ears: The Authentic Story Of a Vital Invention." February 10, 1986.

Yeaton, Barbara. "Chester Greenwood Day to Be Celebrated." *Lewiston Daily Sun*, November 3, 1986.

Books

Porter, Nancy. *Chester . . . More than Earmuffs: A Brief Story of Chester Greenwood*. Wilton, Maine: Wilton Printed Products, 2007.

Weatherford, Doris. *Women in American Politics: History and Milestones, Volume 1*. Thousand Oaks, California: CQ Press, 2012.

Acknowledgments

Thank you to the Maine State Museum, the Maine Historical Society, and the Chamber of Commerce of Farmington, Maine, for their help in finding the photographs for this book.